Essential Skills for a [

MW00341287

Book 3

Let's Go!

Enjoy Companionable Walks
with your Brilliant Family Dog

Beverley Courtney

Books by the author

Essential Skills for a Brilliant Family Dog

Book 1 Calm Down! *Step-by-Step to a Calm, Relaxed, and Brilliant Family Dog*

Book 2 Leave It! *How to teach Amazing Impulse Control to your Brilliant Family Dog*

Book 3 Let's Go! *Enjoy Companionable Walks with your Brilliant Family Dog*

Book 4 Here Boy! *Step-by-step to a Stunning Recall from your Brilliant Family Dog*

Essential Skills for your *Growly* but Brilliant Family Dog

Book 1 Why is my Dog so Growly? *Teach your fearful, aggressive, or reactive dog confidence through understanding*

Book 2 Change for your Growly Dog! *Action steps to build confidence in your fearful, aggressive, or reactive dog*

Book 3 Calm walks with your Growly Dog *Strategies and techniques for your fearful, aggressive, or reactive dog*

www.brilliantfamilydog.com/books

Your free book is waiting for you!

Get the next piece of the puzzle

Get the second book in this series absolutely free at

www.brilliantfamilydog.com/freebook

Disclaimer

I have made every effort to make my teachings crystal clear, but we're dealing with live animals here (That's you, and your dog.) and I can't see whether you're doing it exactly right. I am unable to guarantee success, as it depends entirely on the person utilising the training programs, strategies, tools, and resources.

What I do know is that this system works!

Nothing in these books should upset or worry your dog in any way, but if your dog has a pre-existing problem of fear or aggression you should consult a force-free trainer to help. www.brilliantfamilydog.com/growly will get you started.

By the way, to simplify matters I refer to our trainee dog throughout this series as "she." "He" and "she" will both learn the exact same way. The cumbersome alternatives of "he/she" or "they" depersonalise our learner: I want her to be very real to you!

All the photos in this book are of "real" dogs – either my own, or those of students and readers (with their permission). So the reproduction quality is sometimes not the best. I have chosen the images carefully to illustrate the concepts – so we'll have to put up with some fuzziness.

Contents

Introduction
Oh no! Not again!

Don't walk behind me; I may not lead.
Don't walk in front of me; I may not follow.
Just walk beside me and be my friend.

- Anonymous

This walk is no fun!

You're ready for your daily walk. You are full of hope because you know today is going to be the day your dog walks nicely beside you without pulling your arm out of its socket. You are deluded. Yep, it's going to be just the same as usual.

Lead on = Carthorse mode.

She nearly pulls you over as you step over the threshold. She strains away from you while you try to lock the door. You reach the roadside, and it's head down, PULL! She's choking and spluttering, she's scrabbling along the pavement. She's lurching and weaving - this is no fun for either of you!

I know you've tried lots of gadgets and methods to try to make things better - things suggested by people in the park, by friends, family members, and even trainers - some against your better judgment. But why aren't any of them working? You've got collars and leads to beat the band - some of them designed to inflict pain or make holes in your dog's neck. These devices are sold to prevent pulling, but they just seem to encourage her to pull harder.

I'm guessing that you have been trying to teach your dog *not* to pull. This is sadly doomed to failure. If there's one thing dogs don't understand, it's *not* doing something.

Dogs are doers. They do things. They can't *not* do something. It makes no sense to them. What we have to do is show them something else to do *instead of pulling*.

Many people - and probably you too - have successfully taught their dog not to jump up for a treat by simply hanging on to the morsel until the dog is sitting. She can't jump and sit at the same time, so the jumping dies out.

We can use the exact same system for teaching your dog to walk nicely beside you on a loose lead. Like sitting when a treat is on offer, keeping the lead loose becomes the default behaviour for your dog when she's walking with you. She can't pull ahead and be by your leg at the same time, so the pulling dies out.

Really, yes! It will work for you too!

I've taught this system to hundreds of puppies and dogs, and I'm always amazed at how quickly the dog gets it - once the owner gets it!

You don't need any funny gadgets or kit - though I do have help for extreme *kamikaze* pullers - and there is no force, coercion, or intimidation involved. You're not telling your dog, "You'll do this because I say so." You're saying, "You do this because you like doing it."

You got a dog to be your companion, not to fight with. You wanted to enjoy the great outdoors. You wanted a reason to get out every day to meet people, to visit new places, to get fit, and maybe shift a few pounds.

None of this is going to happen if your walks are a tussle and a misery!

There is much more at stake here than just the health of your shoulders. You'll find endless reasons to put off a walk if it's such hard work. Not only will those pounds pile back on, but your dog will be under-stimulated and under-exercised - and that's a recipe for a dog looking for trouble!

It was having to learn the techniques to make a Brilliant Family Dog with my own busy household of multiple dogs, cats, sheep, goats, hens, and children that set me on the road to helping others do the same. I learnt early on that forcing someone to do something only resulted in grudging compliance at best; whereas getting them to participate and enjoy the process turned them into eager and fast learners. This applied equally to the dogs, the goats - and the children! The sheep and the cats not so much.

My qualifications range from the understanding of learning theory to specialist work for fearful, anxious, and growly dogs. Acquiring an anxious, growly dog of my own ensured that I learnt and understood the process of assimilating the dog into our world in a way which builds her confidence.

There are some superb teachers and advocates of force-free dog training, and you'll find those I am particularly indebted to in the Resources section at the end of this book. Some of the methods I'll be showing you are well-known in the force-free dog training community, while many have my own particular twist.

My work revolves around puppies, new rescue dogs, growly dogs - and, of course, dog owners. There are many people more gifted than I who can train animals to do astonishing things. My gift lies in being able to convey my knowledge to the dog's caregiver in a way which has them saying, "It's so obvious when you put it like that!"

Dogs are individuals and so are their owners, so sometimes creativity and imagination are needed to solve a problem. There isn't a one-size-fits-all approach to training - as you'll see when you look at the Troubleshooting sections following each lesson in the book.

Follow the steps that I outline for you. Don't skip or jump ahead. Work on each step till it's more or less right, then move on. There's no need to be a perfectionist here. You don't want to get stuck.

I suggest you read the whole book before you start so you yourself are clear what you need and what you are aiming for. Then re-read the lesson you're working on and go straight into your very short session. After this you can assess where you are and check the Troubleshooting for any difficulties that relate to you and your dog. Then you're ready for your next session the next day.

So stay with me, follow the directions, don't expect instant miracles, and we'll start changing your walks to comfortable, companionable outings. Most importantly, you will get the companion dog you wanted all along.

Chapter 1
Equipment that will help you…and equipment to avoid like the plague

Coco is choosing to trot along beside me with no pressure on his neck

I'm going to show you not only what equipment you need, but also what equipment you *don't need*, and - importantly! - what equipment to avoid at all costs.

First of all, let's take a quick diversion into anatomy. There is a myth that a dog's neck is somehow different from ours and can withstand the crushing effect of a collar cutting into the throat without any damage whatsoever. This is clearly nonsense. You only have to hear a dog choking as he heaves into his collar or see his eyeballs sticking out, his tongue going blue, and his face creased with the strain to know how wrong this myth is.

In fact, physiologically a dog's neck is *virtually identical to ours*. The trachea, thyroid gland, and oesophagus are all in much the same place. The nerves and blood supply to the brain are similar.

Now, imagine a constricting force on your own neck. What's going to be affected? Your eyes, your throat, your thyroid. lack of blood to the head, distress, fear, pain, and a feeling of being trapped and threatened. Some of these things are temporary, but some can have a permanent effect, and while the damage can be physical, mental damage will also be caused by this pain and aggravation, resulting in stress and anxiety.

Every time this happens, your dog is making a firm association that "walking on a lead means pain and bad things."

So if it's so bad, why on earth do dogs do it?

Dogs, as you'll hear me say repeatedly, are simple creatures. As I said before, they are doers, and they do what works. They aren't straining to pull you somewhere because they have a secret agenda or want to show you who's boss. They are pulling into their collar because they want to get somewhere and you usually follow them!

When they're very young, they don't have to pull that hard for the indulgent owner to stretch out an arm and follow. How often do you think they have to try this before it's a habit? Once? Twice? How often does a child need to see where the chocolate is kept to know which kitchen cupboard to head for? Once, I'd say!

When the dog gets a bit older, larger, and stronger, his owner becomes less forgiving, and he has to pull a lot harder. Sooner or later the pulling wears down the owner's resolve, and they follow their dog. This is why the lead responsiveness and parking exercises you'll find in the Key Lead Skills are so important to work on. You don't need to pull the lead or yank it. Just don't follow!

But my dog is big and strong!

Your dog doesn't need to be large to damage your shoulders with his pulling. A small and determined terrier can exert a lot of force on the lead. If you have a dog who already pulls like a train as soon as the lead is clipped on, then you'll need to dress her in something different while you train her to walk nicely on her collar.

Collars are very useful for attaching ID tags and for quickly holding onto in the heat of the moment, but they aren't essential dog gear. Your dog can wear a harness whenever you're out - provided it's the right kind - or, of course, your dog can wear both.

Collars

Some dogs don't like their collar being touched. They've been hauled about on the collar or dragged somewhere they didn't want to go. I'm horrified when I see people literally dragging a fearful and reluctant puppy along behind them on his bum!

Keep this in mind if you have a rescue dog: rescue dogs may have had a boatload of unpleasant experiences and can be very hand-shy. You might see this as they duck and dive when a hand reaches out toward them. They may also try to grab the hand with their teeth or just freeze in position.

You need to start by changing your dog's view of a collar-hold to a thing of beauty, not fear. Here's an exercise you can do repeatedly, perhaps when you're relaxing after dinner. Keep it brief and fun.

The Collar Hold

1. Reach towards your dog's neck, withdraw your hand again, and then with your other hand give her a tasty treat. Repeat till she's happy with your hand coming towards her neck. She shouldn't flinch or try to grab your hand.

2. Touch your dog's collar, take hand away, and give her a treat. Repeat.

3. Slip your finger into the collar, *remove your hand*, and give her a treat. Repeat.

4. Put your hand through the collar so that the back of your hand is against your dog's neck. You are not gripping the collar. Give her a treat. Remove your hand. Repeat.

5. Walk with your dog beside you. Have your hand through her collar but don't use it to pull her - treat.

6. Repeat each step till your dog is comfortable with it - this may take minutes, days, or even weeks. In time your dog should see your hand approaching and offer her collar to you, then stay still while you slip your hand in, with the back of your hand resting against her neck.

Do buy or use:

The collar should be comfortable to wear, easy to put on and take off, and quick-drying if your dog enjoys swimming. It can be soft webbing, soft leather, or woven fabric - this last is especially useful for puppies as you slot the fabric onto the buckle wherever you want.

I prefer snap collars to buckle collars because you can adjust the size millimetre by millimetre instead of being stuck with pre-punched holes.

Martingale collars made of soft webbing are particularly useful for sighthounds, bull breeds, and any other dog whose neck is larger than its head. These slip over the head and can fit very loosely on the dog's neck - but once the lead is attached they are impossible to back out of. Adjust this collar carefully, fitting it so it doesn't tighten and constrict the neck. It's not meant to be a choke collar.

Any piece of equipment is only as strong as its weakest part - so check clips, fabric, stitching, the soldering on rings, and so on, before you buy. Don't go cheap.

Don't buy or use:

Avoid collars that work by hurting. This includes prong collars, slip collars, chain collars, half-chain collars, choke collars, and *anything* that uses a battery. If you have any of these in your armoury, please destroy them - don't pass them on for some other hapless dog. (An exception to the no-battery rule is the "buzz" collar for deaf dogs, which vibrates like your mobile phone and serves to catch their attention.)

Remember your dog's neck is just as delicate and sensitive as your own neck. Or your child's neck. Thankfully more and more countries are making these instruments of torture illegal.

Harness

Do buy or use:

The harness I personally favour is the *Wiggles Wags and Whiskers Freedom Harness*, listed in the Resources section at the end of this book along with a link to a demo video. You are not so much looking for something to prevent pulling, rather you want a harness designed to promote balance. You are looking for a harness which attaches to a double connection lead in two places - in front and on the back. You want a harness that does not impede shoulder movement, does not chafe or rub, and has the effect of balancing your dog.

The object of using a harness is to prevent the dog pulling into a collar and damaging herself. It can also make Loose Lead Walking a doddle, as the dog has to support herself on her own four feet - without using you as a fifth leg - but it has to be the right sort of harness! Look for one which has the same effect as the one shown in the video.

Don't buy or use:

Some harnesses are designed to encourage the animal to pull, like a horse in harness pulling a cart or a husky pulling a sled. They aren't unpleasant: they're just not the right tool for this job. Others are sold to prevent pulling. Sadly many of these work by hurting the dog - by cutting under the armpits or by tightening and staying tight. Your dog will soon be pulling through the pain just as with her collar.

Head Halters

These require some skill to use humanely, but are useful if your dog continually has her nose on the ground. If the dog lurches to the end of the lead and is stopped abruptly, the head collar could cause her head to twist. It's essential that the lead stays loose when she's wearing it, and you don't flick or jerk it. Gentle pressure to turn the head is what you need but it can take a bit of practice. The best way is to slide your hand right down to where the lead clips onto the head collar and move the dog's head from there. This will ensure you don't yank the lead.

Do buy or use:

Only use a "fixed" head halter (example, *Gentle Leader*). Some figure-of-eight head collars will relax as soon as the pulling stops and are safe to use.

Don't buy or use:

A slip halter, or slip collar-halter combination - all of which tighten and stay tight if the dog pulls.

Leads

Leads are much more important than you may think!

Perhaps you see your lead as a controlling device, a way to move or restrain your dog. What we are working on here is to give the control to the dog, so she can exercise *self-control*. We want her to have the choice to keep the lead loose. Revolutionary, I know! So think of the lead as a connection between you and your dog - as well as insurance that she won't end up under a bus.

In order to give your dog the freedom to walk easily beside you, the lead must be long enough. Six feet is a good length. If the lead is too short, as soon as she moves an inch she's on a tight lead! Most leads you find in pet shops are ridiculously short - three feet or so.

When you're holding the lead, break that habit of winding it five times around your hand then continually flicking and jerking it! Many people have no idea that they're doing this, but every flick or jab is another nail in the coffin of your relationship with your dog.

The lead should be held loosely in your sensitive hand. If you need to prevent yourself jabbing the lead, tuck your thumb into your belt or pocket to keep it still.

If you have to keep your dog on-lead all the time, you'll also do well with a 15-foot long line for when you're in an open space or field. Don't use this line when you're on the road! This length is comfortable to handle and gives your dog the freedom to mooch about and snuffle without danger of her running off. It's important to "flake the line" in your hand - to have it in loose bows or figures-of-eight instead of coils that can tighten and trap a finger. It's the same system sailors use for the rope attached to a fishing net - so that it can pay out freely without getting caught, or catching a leg in a loop and taking a sailor overboard with it.

Do buy or use:

You want a soft fabric or leather lead, at least six feet in length. The lead needs to be light and comfortable to hold in your hands with no sharp edge to the webbing. A multipoint lead where you can adjust the length of the lead is very useful.

A long line of around 15 feet is easiest to handle. There are longer ones, but they're more useful to leave trailing for recall work.

Don't buy or use:

What you do *not* want are extendable leads, bungee leads, anything made with chain, cheap sharp-edged webbing, or a lead less than four feet in length.

Why no extendable lead? These contraptions actually teach the dog to pull! Every time she pulls, she gets more lead. There are also several safety issues around them. I know of cases where the mechanism has broken and the puppy has run into the road and been run over. I also know of cases where people have sustained serious burns to their legs or hands - and in one case, their neck - by the cord racing through the mechanism with a heavy speeding dog on the end. And then there are the dogs who panic when the clumpy plastic handle is dropped and bounces along the road behind them as they flee into danger.

The worst thing is that there is no sensitivity or sense of connection with a plastic handle. It's a lazy and ineffective option.

Devices used by the Inquisition

By now I hardly need tell you to ditch anything that uses fear or intimidation to get results. So into the bin goes anything you throw at your dog, rattle at her, squirt at her, or anything which uses a battery. *

Please destroy these things - don't pass them to another dog owner!

This is a companion you want to enjoy walks with, not an enemy who has to be kept under control with threats and abuse!

When I've explained how leads and collars work to the owners of a dog I'm working with, I'm always pleased when they tell me they've put all the inappropriate items in the bin - so that no-one in the family can use them again on their family pet.

* This specifically excludes the excellent Manners Minder aka Treat-and-Train, which delivers a treat remotely to your dog to mark good behaviours at a distance from you; also "buzz" vibrating collars for deaf dogs.

What's a clicker and do I have to use one?

A clicker is a little gadget you hold in your hand and click to mark the very second your dog is doing something you like. The click is always followed by a treat. It's an excellent way of teaching - especially teaching complex behaviours.

But no, you don't need to use one. If you want to work on more complex behaviours with a clicker at some stage, do a bit of reading up on it first to make sure that you do it right. For now, your hands are going to be full enough with lead, treats, and perhaps gloves if it's cold, so don't worry about it.

You should still mark something you like, though! Marking gives the dog the precise information of what it was that earned her a reward and what she needs to do in order to get rewarded again.

Just as effective at indicating your pleasure at what your dog is doing is to say, "YES!" enthusiastically. Say it quickly, the instant she does the thing you like.

Treats

Here we reach one of the most important pieces of equipment!

Your dog needs to know just what you like and just what does not cut it. Every time she does something you like, you can mark it ("YES!") and give her a treat.

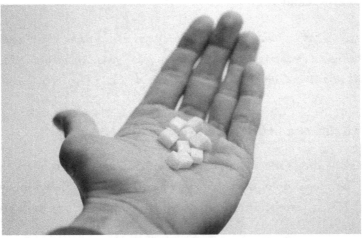

Your dog is going to love these little cubes of tasty cheese!

Good treats

- Cheese
- Sausage
- Ham
- Chicken
- Frankfurter
- Salami
- Homemade sardine, tuna, or ham cookies
- Freeze-dried 100% meat treats
- Dehydrated liver, heart, lung, etc.

…real food in other words. Ideally, they slip down quickly so your dog wants more. Cut them into small, pea-size treats.

OK treats

- High-quality grain-free commercial treats

Fairly rubbish treats

- Your dog's usual kibble (She gets it anyway. Why should she have to work for it?)
- Cat biscuits
- Dog biscuits
- Stuff of unrecognisable composition sold as pet treats
- Anything you wouldn't put in your own mouth

Do you work more enthusiastically for £60 an hour or for 50p an hour? Quite so. Your dog is the same. Be sure the treats you're offering are worth working for!

Troubleshooting

Why do I have to keep giving my dog treats? Shouldn't he do what he's told anyway?

I only give my dogs a treat when they've done something I like. I aim to get through a lot of treats every day! Treats are not a moral issue. They are a means to an end. The end is your dog walking willingly beside you on a loose lead. If employing a few bits of cheese means that my walks are enjoyable and my shoulder will not need rehab, then that seems a good deal to me.

But isn't all this extra food bad for him?

You're using high-quality food for treats. It's not like giving chocolate to a child. You have to feed your dog anyway, so you may as well get some mileage from it. If your dog tends to be overweight, simply remove an equivalent amount of food from his dinner.

Can I carry on using my present equipment?

Nope, not if it isn't on the approved list above! Make life easy for yourself and get the right tools for the job.

I use a short lead, because she always pulls to the end of it anyway.

Not any more, she won't. Once you've perfected the exercises in Chapter 2 she'll know that it's her job to keep the lead loose. A 6 or 8-foot lead will give her that opportunity, and you won't be following her! We'll be getting down to the nitty-gritty in the next chapter. You have to build the foundations first, and giving your dog the freedom to choose is an essential part of that.

What's wrong with extendable leads?

They're dangerous, insensitive, difficult to control, and unreliable. They actually teach your dog to pull! There is no connection between you if you're holding a lump of plastic attached to a thin cord. What do you think a top showjumper would say if you told him he had to hold a plastic handle instead of feel his horse's reins between his fingers? You'll be learning more lead skills in this book which will give you amazing control with the lightest of touches.

In this section we have discovered:

- It's vital to get the right equipment to make your walks enjoyable
- It's critical to stop using anything that causes stress, anxiety, or pain
- To teach your dog to love having her collar held
- "I'm paid to keep my lead loose - now I get it!"

Chapter 2
Change your mindset first

Coco strides out proudly, knowing exactly where he's meant to be

This is not a case of "them and us". We're talking about going for a companionable walk with your doggy best friend.

First of all, imagine going for a walk with your human best friend. You'd walk together and probably fall into step. You may hold hands or link arms. You'd chat and laugh. You'd point things out to each other as you pass them. You may interrupt your conversation to say, "Look at this flower," and you'll both wander over to examine it. Your friend may say, "What's in that shop window over there?" and you both - arm in arm - go to study it.

This is a pleasant walk. This is what you want to aspire to with your dog. So the first thing to do is change your mindset from having an adversarial outing to a companionable one.

This includes allowing your dog the opportunity to be a dog.

Unless you've got a train to catch, your walk can have many sniff-points. It's a chance for you both to unwind and explore your surroundings. Your dog will point out to you lots of things you never noticed before! You don't have to go 100 yards this way, turn left, 300 yards that way, turn right... etc. You can just go where the fancy takes you. You'll get your exercise just the same, don't worry!

Now I hear you cry: "But that's not what it's like! My arm is being ripped out of its socket! He has no interest in me!" So let's start from the beginning.

Holding the lead

The lead is not a gadget for restraining your dog, nor a device for hauling you along! The lead is there to keep your dog from running under a bus, possibly to help with her self-control when she wants to greet someone, and, *most importantly*, it's a connection between the two of you. Messages go up and down this lead. Keeping it tight with a vice-like grip will prevent any communication.

Go back to the walk with your friend. Do you grip his hand so tight it hurts? Do you yank him over to look at your flower? Does he turn on his heel without a word and haul you over to the shop window?

No! You're enjoying a walk together.

The same is true of you and your dog, and changing your view of the lead is the first thing to do. It may surprise - nay, astonish! - you to learn that if you keep the lead loose, your dog will keep it loose too.

It takes two to tango, as the saying goes, and it takes two to have a tight lead.

One of us has to stop pulling, and as we're the ones with the bigger brains, it needs to be us. Sadly, this pulling has often started in puppyhood and is now an entrenched habit. When people have their cute new little puppy, they tend to let it pull them all over the place. They think it is kind.

It is not kind.

It's teaching the puppy to damage her throat and neck as you saw in Chapter 1, and to ignore the person on the other end of the lead. So they have their pup on a lead. The puppy pulls towards something. Their arm stretches out. The puppy pulls harder. With outstretched arm they follow the puppy.

What has this puppy just learnt? "If I pull, they'll follow. And if I pull harder, they'll follow faster."

For some reason that escapes me, people find this appealing. Once the pup has grown a few months and can get some traction and force, not so much.

You never have to pull your dog's lead again!

Here's an exercise for you to change this entirely. You can do it in the kitchen first, then graduate to the garden before trying it on the road.

Key Lead Skill No.1
Holding the Lead

1. Have your dog on a longish lead (at least 2 metres)

2. Stand still and let the dog pull to the end of the lead, wherever she wants to go

3. Keep your hand close to your hip. Tuck your thumb into your belt if necessary

4. *Wait.* Wait till the lead slackens the tiniest bit. It doesn't matter why. You may think you'll need to wait forever, but it's usually only 20 seconds or so at most

5. As soon as you feel the lead relax - for any reason at all - call your dog and reward her with a tasty treat at your knee

6. Repeat till she understands that it's up to her to keep the lead loose

This exercise is simplicity itself. It tells your dog that you are no longer the one that's pulling. Your hands are soft. It's her choice if she pulls. Given a little time, she'll choose not to pull at all.

If your dog is in the habit of lurching to the end of the lead as soon as it's on, you may have to repeat this exercise frequently. In most cases we need repeat it only long enough to get the new system of lead-holding *into our own heads*. Once we've got it, our dog will get it.

Remember, dogs are doers, not not-doers. So your dog is learning to keep the lead loose, rather than not to pull on it. See the difference?

What you accept is what you get

Every time you put the lead on your dog, you need to remember to keep your hand close to you and *wait* for her to slacken the lead. If you are in the habit of putting on the lead and letting your dog pull you to the door, then that is what will happen.

What you reward is what you get.

There are few better rewards for most dogs then heading out through that door! Your dog needs to learn that - no matter what happened in the past - things have now changed, which means pulling on the lead will get her nowhere. Dogs aren't dumb. They do what works.

From now on you will never move until the lead is slack.

NEVER!

If you find your arm floating out, recapture it and tuck it into your belt! If it keeps happening, put one of your children on "arm-watch." They'll love having the chance of pointing out your mistake to you!

Time to keep still

Once your dog has learnt to keep that lead loose, and stay more or less near you, you can start on the next Key Lead Skill. It's incredibly useful and keeps your dog calmly under control without any effort from either of you.

If you want to stop and chat to someone, make a purchase in a shop, or wait at a bus stop, you can put the handbrake on and park your dog. This is a great way to immobilise your dog without any vestige of force or anger. This is how you do it:

Key Lead Skill No.2
Parking

1. The first thing is to hold your dog's collar. Rather than waving your arm about trying to catch the collar on a leaping dog, simply run your hand down the lead till you reach the collar, and slip a finger under it.

2. While holding the collar (gently!), allow the lead to fall to the floor and stand on it right beside your dog's front paw. Hang on to the handle all the while.

3. Now you can let go of the collar, straighten up, and keep holding on to that handle. A 6-foot lead is ideal for this.

4. Ignore your dog. No more interaction between you.

Your dog can take any position she likes. She's simply unable to pull or jump up. Your hands are free to delve into your purse or drink a coffee. Your visitor is safe from being jumped on. Your dog will find that as nothing more is happening, sitting or lying down is a good option.

When you get fluent and quick at parking, you'll have a way to anchor your dog easily. Be sure to hold the collar before trying to stand on the lead or you'll find yourself doing the can-can as your dog flies forward while you try to get your foot on a waving lead!

Before we move on, let's take a look at what's buzzing around in your head.

Troubleshooting

This doesn't work. My dog still pulls like a train, choking and spluttering.

Hang on! We're only at the foundation stage. You're building a different response in your dog's mind: it takes time. Keep working on these two exercises several times a day till your dog becomes as light as a feather on the end of the lead. For saner walks meanwhile, have a look at Chapter 1, where we discussed the pros and cons of various gadgets sold to aid Loose Lead Walking. There'll be something there to help you improve your walks humanely.

Do I have to give my dog treats?

Oh yes! We give treats to the dog to show her that we like what she just did. This means she will do it again. Why would you want to stop this sequence? The treats need to be good ones! Not manky old cat biscuits and fluff from the depths of your pocket, but what a friend of mine terms "crack cocaine cookies" - small chunks of beefburger, garlic sausage, ham, cheese, dried liver - irresistible morsels that are worth working for.

It's ok till we see another dog or person then all hell lets loose.

Chapter 3 will come to the rescue, but don't skip ahead! It's important to establish the foundation skills. We're just beginning. Don't expect miracles -

just yet! It may have taken your dog years to get to this level of lead-pulling expertise, so it won't change overnight.

I'm waiting for her to stop pulling, but she just keeps on. How long should I wait?

Wait till she stops. I know you think you'll both be standing there till Christmas - but really, it's more like a few seconds. If you're very close to something - for example, if you are nose to nose with another dog - then this is too hard and you'll need to back off. Methods for doing this without hauling your dog backwards in the upcoming chapters.

If I stop every time she pulls, we'll take forever to get anywhere.

Too true, but you're not trying to get anywhere yet. You're teaching your dog that it's up to her to keep the lead loose. This is an essential first step, so keep working on it at every opportunity.

He's ok with me, but the children nearly get pulled over.

If you have a dog who pulls hard or who is unpredictable (that's most of them), it's not appropriate for a child to be walking him. Depending on the size of the dog and the maturity of the child, you may be able to supervise walks with your child holding the lead when he hits early teenage years. Safety is key. I taught my children never to put their hand through the handle of the lead and to let go of the lead if the dog pulled. I'd rather have a run-over dog than a run-over dog and a run-over child. But I never let them get into such a situation.

I shout at her to stop pulling, but she ignores me.

She probably thinks you're egging her on! Here's the thing: dogs do *not* understand negative concepts. They are doers. They need to be doing something. *They can't not do anything.* So we are going to reframe the whole adventure into a "do this" format, instead of a "don't do that" one. Stay with me - it'll become clear!

We've hardly begun and you have learnt

- To honour your dog so you can enjoy walking together with her
- To hold the lead in such a way that you *never* have to pull the lead ever again
- To keep your dog stationary without shouting, intimidation, pushing, or pulling
- "Wow! My throat's not hurting any more!"

Chapter 3
If she's not out front, where should she be?

This is the Reward Spot. Coco knows just where to be to earn his reward

We've established that dogs can't *not do something*. They have to *do something*.

We're going to start by showing your dog where we'd like her to be when we are moving. She has to know where to be in order to be there!

Choose which side you'd like your dog to walk and stick to that side for the time being. It doesn't matter which side. It simply makes everything much easier for *you* to learn while you get your mechanics right. She can walk either side in a few weeks once you've got it.

It's you who has to do some learning here. Just like driving a car, if you grate the gears and stamp on the pedals your car is not going to perform well. To get a smooth "drive" with your dog, you're going to need to learn these Key Lead Skills carefully. Your dog will say, "Oh, *that's* what she wants!" and it will all become a breeze.

Let's say you want to walk your dog on your left side - I'll give you directions for that. If you prefer the dog on your right side, just reverse all the lefts and rights below! So you'll be holding your lead and your treats in your right hand. Your left hand will stay empty (no lead, no treat).

To show her where she should be when she's on lead, we'll teach her the Reward Spot. Whenever she's there, she'll get a treat. It's the place she has to be to get us to move forward - that spot is by your left leg, with her head at your trouser seam.

Don't get tangled up with the details - just remember that this is a game you're playing with your dog: you're challenging her to catch you up at your left leg no matter what you may do to escape!

Lesson 1: Teaching your dog to find the Reward Spot

1. Start this in a quiet place - my dogs all learn this in the kitchen! To begin with, a one-minute session is good. Always keep these sessions very, very short.

2. Stand with your dog roughly on your left. Your lead will be held loosely in your right hand with a big loop reaching almost to the floor in a J-shape. Have 10-15 tasty treats in your cupped right hand. Turn a bit so your dog has a good chance of reaching your left side first, wherever she's coming from.

3. As your dog comes towards you, say, "YES" *Then* take a treat with your left hand, touch your hand to your left trouser seam at dog nose height - this is your Reward Spot - and feed the treat to her as she arrives.

4. Take one step away to the right and wait for her to look at you or move towards you - "YES!" - down comes another treat to your trouser seam and into her mouth!

5. To begin with, she won't be that close to your leg, just paying attention. The gap between her and you will gradually close as she wants to get that treat.

6. Repeat this till she realises that getting close to your left leg produces a treat: take a single step away from her (sideways, backwards, or occasionally forwards). Keep this speedy, rhythmical, and fun. After a while you'll find it hard to get away from her! She's saying, "Ha! You can't catch me out!" and whooshing into your left leg.

7. At this stage it doesn't matter which way your dog is facing, and it doesn't matter if she jumps up or paws you. Just wait for her feet to hit the floor before you reach for the treat.

8. If she gets lost or confused, coming into the wrong side, or if she wraps the lead round you, just do a quick 180 degree turn to unravel her. Give her the greatest chance of success at hitting your left leg.

9. Make it as easy as possible for her to succeed. *We're teaching, not testing.* You may need to keep turning to ensure she hits the correct side and learns where that Reward Spot is. "Ooh, you clever girl!" you can say, as you turn so that she finds herself on your left side.

Watchpoints

- Don't hold the treat out to lure her to come to you: "Please, doggy. Please!" Don't beg her! Wait for her to work it out. *After you've said, "YES,"* you fetch a treat from your other hand, touch it to your leg, and feed. She may be slow to catch on at first, but once she knows you have food, she just has to figure out how to get it. You may need to keep both hands together to prevent one slipping down your leg before she's got there!

- Always touch the treat-hand to your leg. What we're teaching is technically a Nose Target - telling our dogs, "When your nose is close to my leg, you get a treat." Those of you who've read the first book in this series, *Calm Down! Step-by-step to a Calm, Relaxed, and Brilliant Family Dog,* will recognise the concept of targets - in that case, when getting your dog to land on her mat it was a <u>paw</u> target - now it's a <u>nose</u> target. When you call your family down to dinner, they don't wander off into the garage or to the front gate, they come to the table! That's where the food arrives. So touching the treat to your leg at dog-nose-height means that that's where she'll come to get it every time. If you make a mistake and feed straight to her mouth, she won't have this certainty about where exactly she should be. Six inches away? A foot away? A yard away? Make this crystal clear, and it will be much easier for your dog!

- A large dog will be very close to your side, with her Reward Spot at your hip. A small dog may stay a little further out from your leg to avoid being trodden on and to be able to see your face. Her Reward Spot will be much nearer the floor! If you have a problem bending this far, smear some pure peanut butter, liver pate, or squeezy cheese onto a wooden spoon and hold that down by your ankle for a quick lick each time you've said, "YES," then lift it up again.

- Be sure to keep the lead loosely in your right hand - the opposite side from the dog - and looping down in a nice J-shape that allows your dog freedom. Be careful not to flick or tighten the lead. The plan here is for your dog to stay by your left leg because she wants to be there. She's not there because you make her. It has to be her choice!

- Be sure to feed with your left hand - same side as your dog. If you feed with your right hand, you will be quite unable to touch your food hand to your left trouser seam - making the Reward Spot a fuzzy area - and you'll be drawing your dog round in front of you. You want her head level with your leg.

- Only take *one step* in any direction - we're not walking yet! We're just establishing the position to be in when the lead is on. Don't jump ahead!

- If you're finding this confusing, try without the dog. Really! Just like dancers have to get their steps right on their own before trying with a partner or a group, you can get the lead and treats into the correct hand, imagine what your dog is doing, then run through a few goes. This may help you get your mechanics down.

Dogs learn by rhythm and patterning. The more rhythmic and fluent (and quick!) you can make your session, the faster she'll learn.

Once you've got it, your dog will get it very quickly.

Your first tentative steps

You may need to take a week or more teaching your dog her Reward Spot. Have at least one - preferably two or three - one-minute sessions every day. Every time you put the kettle on is a good time for a session, or every time you've been to the bathroom. You can build a habit that makes it very easy to fit your training into your already busy day. You can encourage your dog to find the Reward Spot whenever you call her - just turn as she's arriving and touch the treat to your trouser seam. This is her new Best Place Ever!

Up to now, having her nose near the Reward Spot has been enough to earn a treat regardless of where the rest of her body is. Once she's hitting that spot every time, we need to let her find the Reward Spot in such a way that she ends up the right way round.

Here you go:

Lesson 2: Reward Spot on the Move

1. Do a few treats' worth of Reward Spot as usual, just moving *one step* away from your dog in any direction. Make sure she always stays on your left side - help her if necessary by turning your body. Don't test her by getting her the wrong side of you. Softly, softly …

2. Very fluently - *without any break in the rhythm you've built up* - drop a treat just behind your left foot. While your dog is scarfing this up, take one step forward (two steps for anything larger than a collie).

3. Your dog will look up, see you've moved, and rush to catch up with you as you look back over your left shoulder to admire her.

4. As she arrives at your leg - "YES!" - down comes another treat for her, touched to your trouser seam in the reward spot.

5. Instantly, in the same rhythm, place another treat behind your left foot.

Repeat steps 2 to 4, building a fast rhythm. Now your dog is diving for the treat, spinning round and landing next to your left leg - more or less the right way round!

Once you've established the Reward Spot, right on your leg, it's the same whether you are standing, walking, running, hopping, or calling your dog to you.

Instead of a complicated system of Loose Lead Walking, your dog only has to learn this one thing: always be at my person's left side with my nose near their leg. How easy is that? I will be showing you some more games, but basically it's all *Reward Spot on the Move*.

Troubleshooting

My dog doesn't stop at the Reward Spot - she flies ahead!

What enthusiasm! With a fast dog you need to be fast too and anticipate her. As she lifts her head from eating the treat, you say "YES!" By the time the word has come out of your mouth, she should be just passing your leg. She'll look up because you said, "Yes," and get her treat from her Reward Spot. Working in a small circle - with her on the outside - may help to slow her down. Don't worry if she's going past and then coming back to you, facing the wrong direction when she arrives. Practice makes perfect. She'll soon learn that the game goes faster if she stops on the way!

My dog is sniffing around after he's eaten his treat from the floor.

Be sure to use treats that don't crumble. Crumbly biscuit or flaky chicken will cause him to go into search mode every time he puts his nose down. This will teach him to hoover. Soft, slippery treats he can grab in one go then spin round are what you need.

She goes to get the treat, loses the plot, and wanders off.

You may need to ensure the floor is clear of toys and other distractions, but the key here is to establish a rhythm and get it going fast. She should be bouncing into position beside you. If she's distracted by a sound, make a kissy or clucky noise to get her focus back to you. A noise is better than using her name. On no account chide her - or it will no longer be a fun game.

You say to keep the lead loose, but I have to keep it short or she goes too far away.

Then she'll never learn to stay in place of her own volition. You have to give the dog a choice so she can make a good decision (which earns her food) or a poor decision (which earns her nothing at all). If you keep her in place with a short lead, she's limited in her choice, so she can't make a good one! Does that make sense? Persevere with a loopy lead and see how it begins to work when your dog has the freedom to make a mistake. It doesn't matter if at this stage she's bouncing back and forth. She'll settle as the game becomes clear to her.

Why only one step? I want to get moving!

Patience, Grasshopper! You'll be moving soon enough. Imagine you're learning the piano. You don't start with a Beethoven Concerto. You start with simple tunes, scales and exercises to build up your knowledge and ability. If you can get your dog flying into the Reward Spot every time after one step (two steps for larger dogs), you'll be ready for the next stage, but don't be in a hurry to push the supports away - we want a firm foundation so your building stays up!

We had the Reward Spot perfect, but once I take a step we lose the rhythm.

Do what you may have done for learning the Reward Spot and try without the dog. Once you get a rhythm handling the treats, placing one down, and being ready with the next at your leg, you may find your dog trots over and joins in!

He takes the treat from the floor, turns very slowly, and plods up to my leg - where he stops and sits. Is this right?

All dogs are different. Maybe you have a large heavy breed like a Mountain Dog, that do things more slowly than - say, a Working Cocker Spaniel, who do everything at 100 miles an hour. So if that's the fastest he ever goes when walking, then that's fine. If you're only taking two steps, he should arrive with you as soon as he's turned, so doesn't need to follow you - yet. Moving more than two steps will come later. If he wants to sit when he reaches your leg and you're stationary, that's also fine. Some people like to teach a sit every time they stop. This tends to come with practicing the Reward Spot on the Move. If your dog is very dozy and slow, have a quick, short game of chase or retrieve in the garden first to get him engaged with you and more lively. He needs to enjoy the session and not be bored silly!

In this section we have learnt

- How to give your dog a fixed spot where she should always be when on lead
- Showing her how to find that spot when you move
- That rhythm and patterning will establish the habit
- That it's a process of building the understanding - not launching onto the street and expecting your dog to know what you want
- "I like bouncing back and forth! I like being in this spot."

Chapter 4
Keeping those hands soft at all times

Soft hands on the long line, gently turning Meg away from a distraction

Keeping your hands soft on a floppy lead can be hard to do. You've spent ages holding the lead tight as if your life depended on it, restricting your dog's freedom.

Now we want the dog to have freedom - freedom to choose to stay beside us! - so making sure you keep your hands soft and the lead loose is going to go a long way towards this. If your dog sails off away from you, you need to be able to stop her without yanking her off her feet. You want her to slow down, turn, and choose to come back to you. The lead needs to stay fluid so nothing sudden happens.

I know you're thinking if you loosen the lead, she'll pull all the time - but that's the old thinking. You now know that giving your dog the freedom to choose and then rewarding the choice you want will have her making good decisions in no time. As she learns these new skills, things will be changing dramatically before your eyes.

So let's look at how you can slow your dog to a gentle halt without pulling.

You really never have to pull your dog's lead again!

Key Lead Skill No. 3
Slow Stop

1. Your dog is heading away from you, perhaps in pursuit of a good scent, or trying to reach someone.

2. If she walks on your left, you'll have the lead in your right hand. You are using a lead of at least 6 feet in length, aren't you?

3. As she moves away from you, loosely cup your left hand under the lead, letting the lead run through freely, *gradually* closing your grip so she can feel this squeezing action as the lead slows down.

4. This will slow her sufficiently to ease her into a stand.

5. Now relax your hands and lead - you may need to take a small step forward to let your hands relax and drop down - and admire your dog standing on a loose lead.

6. You can attract her back to the Reward Spot with your voice - treat, and carry on.

This should all be calm, mostly noiseless, and easy. It's like holding your friend's hand and gently slowing them down till they come back into step beside you. No need for "Oi!" "Stop!" "C'me here" or anything else other than saying, "Good Girl!" and giving her a welcoming smile when she reorients to you.

Try this first with another person instead of your dog to help you. Ask them to hold the clip of the lead in their hand, turn away from you and let the lead drape over their shoulder, with you holding the end behind them. As they walk away and you start to close your fingers on the lead, they should be fully aware of that sensation and respond to it. They'll be able to tell you very clearly if you're gently slowing them or jolting them to a stop! Your dog too will recognise this feeling on the lead as "Oh hallo, we're stopping now."

When you start, it may take a few attempts to get your dog to stay still and balanced when she stops so that you're able to relax the lead. After a while she'll know that this rubbing sensation on the lead is the precursor to a halt. The right sort of harness will help enormously to get her to balance on her own four feet instead of using you as a fifth leg. See Chapter 1, and the Resources section at the end of the book.

Troubleshooting

My dog stops alright, but as soon as I relax my hands, she surges forward again.

It's good that you've got the slow stop. Now you relax your hands just a little (an inch or so) to test whether she's standing balanced on her own feet. If she immediately starts to lean forward again, ease her to a stop again - maybe just using your fingers on the line - and test again. Sooner or later, she's going to realise that slow stop means stand still.

I can stop her pulling forward but she just stands looking ahead, so I give up and follow her.

You're halfway there! Once you've slow-stopped her and relaxed your hands you can now *wait*. Unless there is something super-attractive just in front of her, sooner or later, she'll look back at you to see if you've died. Now you are doing Key Lead Skill No.1 and can encourage her to your knee for a treat. If you walk her on the left, for instance, that treat can be delivered at her Reward Spot. Now you can go forward. Dogs are clever, but they are not (always) mind readers! Help her.

Sometimes she'll come back to my leg before we go forward again.

There's something you're not telling me here! "Sometimes" she does it perfectly suggests that sometimes she does not and you go forward anyway. This is going to confuse your dog: "Is today one of the days I can pull forward?" She needs to know that pulling on the lead will *never* get forward movement. Now she'll be much faster at coming back to her Reward Spot until she gives up on pulling forward altogether. Can you remember when your mother would say, "What's the magic word?" when you asked for something without a "please"? You soon learnt that saying, "Please," got you what you wanted without that annoying delay! This is a gradual process. It will come. Your task is to be utterly consistent: from now on, whenever your dog is on a lead you are training her!

I've been doing this stop-go stuff for days now, but she still wants to pull forward.

Keep going! This doesn't happen overnight. In a few weeks you'll be surprised how much things have changed. In a year you'll have forgotten she ever pulled at all. If you give up now, she'll carry on pulling happily forever. It takes time practicing it in the house or other distraction-free areas before you can get it to work on the road. And patience - a lot of patience.

You really, really, never have to pull your dog's lead again!

Where this can come unstuck is when your dog pulls away from you and resolutely stays pulling away. You are diligently following the instructions outlined in Chapter 2 for Key Lead Skill No.1 *"You never have to pull your dog's lead again!"* but your dog just stays there, leaning into the lead.

This is probably because she is distracted by something that is so close that she can't shift her mind away from it: another dog right in front of her? Some dropped food? A favourite person approaching?

If you don't like the look of the dog in front of her, the food looks dangerous, or there's a truck driving towards you - you need to be able to move her, fast.

If you try to drag her backwards out of the situation, you are pulling against all the strongest muscles of a dog - her back and haunches. Think of the strength a carthorse exerts to get a cart moving and think how hard it would be to pull against that power.

You need another lead skill so that she turns toward you of her own volition, *without you trying to haul her backwards!* Here it is:

Key Lead Skill No. 4 Lead Stroking

Meg responds to the stroking by turning back to me

1. Your dog is at the end of the lead and too close to the distraction to respond. Maybe you need to move her because of danger or for good manners.

2. Move yourself slightly to one side or the other so that you are in her peripheral vision. Bend towards her in a friendly and playful way. Dogs have 270-degree vision as opposed to our 180 degrees, so you don't have to move far.

3. While making clucky, cooing noises - don't bark her name - start stroking the lead gently.

4. Use a hand-over-hand action, as if you were pulling a rope in - but *you are not pulling*, just stroking! Your stroking action would be the same pressure you might use to stroke a baby's hand.

5. Watch her collar or harness to ensure that you are not tightening the lead and pulling.

6. As you stroke and make super-attractive noises, your dog will look round, see you, and start to turn towards you.

7. Engage her eyes with yours, happily congratulating her, and back away a few steps, still bending forwards.

8. As soon as she's disconnected from the distraction you can turn and carry on walking.

9. You can give her a treat as you trot away, telling her how good she is.

You *never* have to pull your dog's lead again.

Troubleshooting

I'm doing all this stroking but she's still pulling ahead. I have no choice but to pull her backwards.

Up your level of enthusiastic "coochy-coos" and the moment her head turns towards you, move backwards while she engages with you and gives you eye contact. Don't turn until you've got this connection. If she's still rivetted on what has distracted her, try walking sideways, perpendicular to her, to make it easier for her to join you before you back off.

This is great! She turns really quickly to join me, but as I jog away she's leaping up beside me.

As long as she's not grabbing your sleeve I'd be delighted with the jumping. It shows you've taught this really well as a game and she's keen to turn from her distraction to play with you. If she wants to grab, have a soft toy ready for her to sink her teeth into.

The very beginnings of your companionable walk

No, you're not heading off for a loose lead walk right now - but you're getting there ...

First I want you to incorporate your new lead skills into your walks, just a little at a time. The more fluent you are, the easier this will be, and the more responsive your dog will become.

If your dog starts to surge, you can choose one of your new Key Lead Skills. You can wait for her to realise she needs to get back to you in order to move forward, you can start to slow down, bringing her to a slow-stop, or - if she's stuck - stroke the lead with kissy noises to draw her back into your world *without pulling!*

You can use your ordinary 6-foot lead for this, or if you're in a larger space you can use your 15-foot line - don't use a long line near a road. I'd recommend you walk your dog on a harness for now, too. The right sort will remove a lot of stress from both of you! See Chapter 1 and the Resources Section at the end of the book for guidance on the right harness to get.

Troubleshooting

My puppy doesn't pull - she just sits down and won't budge! I don't like dragging her along the pavement.

Please don't drag your puppy along! If she's having a sit-down strike, it could be because she's tired. Young puppies need only minutes walking on a hard surface. If she's not tired, it's most likely because she's anxious about what's ahead. That leaf she saw fluttering in the breeze could be a snake or other monster. The shape ahead she can't identify could be a bottomless pit! As for the motorbike parked at the side of the road - a Martian?! When she sits, just relax your lead and give her time to assess the danger. It's all new to her! After a while she'll look less worried and stop fixating on whatever it is, then you can make your attractive sounds, tickle the lead, and she'll come trotting along with you again. It's an important part of her Habituation and Socialisation process that she has time to study things that may worry her.

My dog wants to sniff the hedge all the way.

Try walking further out from intoxicating smells like the hedgerow. Stop and re-engage him. More techniques for getting his attention on you are in the next chapter, where we'll be taking this on the road!

My dog plods along so slowly behind me.

Breeds are different in their behaviour. My Whippet Cricket likes to walk just behind my feet. Rollo the Border Collie can't get anywhere fast enough! If your dog is a heavy or giant breed, speed may not be his watchword. As long as he's keeping up with you, a slow pace can be enjoyable. If he seems to be labouring, he is not old, and it's not very hot, there are two things to check: he may be overweight, or consider a vet check for nagging joint problems.

My dog is 8 years old and she's always surged out ahead of me. Is there any hope of changing this?

It's clearly a well-established habit, but *yes*, you can change this. Maybe she'll always like to be a bit ahead of you, but that's ok as long as she's not pulling! Follow this system and you can eliminate the pulling.

I've damaged my arm. It's really difficult to hold the lead and the treats.

You'd better use your good arm for the lead and treats for now. Slow things down a bit. If your dog is not huge and doesn't lunge violently, a very good method is to attach the lead to your belt or tie it round your hips, so that you're hands-free. Round the hips is better than round the waist, which can stress your back - your hips are pretty stable. Try this in a safe place to see how it goes. You may find that in addition to resting your arm you are cutting out all the unconscious flicks and jabs you were doing with the lead, and your dog will respond much better!

In this Chapter, we've learnt

- To use two Key Lead Skills to change your dog walking experience for ever
- To exercise patience and gentleness when walking with your dog
- "I'm free to sniff and explore without my neck hurting!"

Chapter 5
Get moving!

Rollo enjoys a pleasant walk with me, his lead loose

- Your dog knows the Reward Spot
- She can find it when you're moving
- You've got the four Key Lead Skills

Now we're going to get moving!

1 2 3 Treat!

If you want, you can just get moving using the Reward Spot, rewarding your dog whenever she's there at your leg and looking at you. For some people this works really well, but most prefer this next stage which really cements all the stages together into a fluent walk. For this, you are going to be counting out loud with each step you take - "1, 2, 3, Treat!" then you stop.

To begin with your dog will have no clue what you're doing, but if you are rhythmic in your stepping and counting, very soon she'll get the message that treats are on offer every fourth step and she will make sure she's beside you when you say "Treat". You are teaching her to check in with you every few steps - what you would expect from a companion on a walk.

Lesson 3: Checking in

1. Get yourself ready with your dog by your side, lead and treats in the opposite hand. Treat her in the Reward Spot so she knows what game you're playing.

2. Start counting *out loud* rhythmically with each step as you walk forward: "1, 2, 3, Treat!"

3. Stand still.

4. If, when you say, "Treat," your dog is there at your leg, you touch the treat to your trouser seam and feed her. If she's wandered off, wait for her to turn back to you, then treat.

5. Immediately step out again, counting. It really is that simple! Don't overcomplicate it.

Troubleshooting

My dog is wandering off before we even start.

Be sure to treat him in the Reward Spot so he knows something is happening. Move quickly into your counting so he hasn't lost interest before you begin.

We start off well, but she keeps going behind me and switching sides.

Keep an eye on her - look down over your shoulder so she can see you and not feel the disconnect that leads to her doing her own thing. This isn't a test! Make it as easy as possible for her to succeed by staying with you - chat to her.

Now she's watching me all the time!

And that's a problem? You've done well to get her to enjoy this game and stay beside you where she can comfortably watch you. Over time you'll both relax and walk more naturally. She doesn't have to watch you like an Obedience Champion, as long as she checks in with you every few steps. Just let it flow for now.

I have to wait ages for her to come back to me. She zips to the end of the lead as soon as I say, "One."

Go back to working the Reward Spot on the Move in Chapter 3, so she remembers she's meant to be by your leg. Once that's going fluently again, just move into this game and start counting. She should be right with you!

Every time I turn she manages to get on the wrong side of me.

I suspect what's happening is that you are walking forward evenly then suddenly, perhaps because you've reached the wall of your room, you spin round. She is caught by surprise, but quickly tries to stay with you - inevitably on the wrong side of you! So instead of walking in straight lines with sharp turns, try to find a space where you can walk in a large circle or oval with your dog on the outside. Maybe your driveway. If you have one of those splendid kitchens with an island, you have a ready-made, purpose-built, Loose Lead Walking training ground!

When do I add my word "Heel!"? She doesn't seem to understand it.

There are two questions here. No dog understands any words until they're taught what they mean. The way to teach a word is to pair the word with the action you want. So you say, "sit" as your dog's bum is going towards the ground, for instance. You need to describe what she's doing while she's doing it - that way she'll make the connection. Having said that, let's look at the other question - about using a vocal cue. I haven't suggested you use a word for loose lead walking at all. The reason? It's a default behaviour which needs no words. The way you stand and hold the lead tells your dog what to do. Dogs pay much more attention to our body language than to what we say. Whenever your dog has the lead attached your motion produces the desired action of keeping her by your leg. You don't need to tell her! I do say, "Let's go!" to my dogs when I'm starting to move - perhaps when we've waited for the traffic to clear to cross the road. This is just to give them some warning that I'm moving. They put themselves in the right place.

She's great up till she gets the treat, then her mind and nose are elsewhere.

This is not uncommon if you lose the rhythm. She thinks she's done the right thing by staying with you till you treated her (and she's right!), but while you pause to think of what to do next she reckons it's over and goes off sniffing. So as soon as you treat, say, "One," and step off smartly. This is where the rhythm is so important. No gaps.

Remember: dogs learn by rhythm and patterning!

You don't need to march like a soldier or take giant steps! Walk naturally, but smartly and rhythmically - just as you do when you're walking with a purpose, as opposed to ambling or shuffling along.

Be careful not to overdo it

As with the other techniques, do just a little at a time to begin with. Don't bore your dog!

You'll find you quickly get fluent at 1, 2, 3, Treat, and you should soon find yourself walking along smartly, your attentive dog at your side! You'll need to adjust your stride and pace slightly to accommodate your dog's size and pace.

A very small dog may need you to take smaller steps to keep with you. A large, rangy dog will require you to stride out manfully.

Find what works for your dog first. It can be hard for a large dog to walk very slowly - she's always having to dot-and-carry-one to stay with you, possibly going sideways at the same time. So stride out and find a pace which works for her. Once you have this going smoothly and fluently, you can start to ease the pace slightly so your dog stays at the same gait while making smaller steps. A trotting dog always works better than a walking dog.

Eventually you'll reach a perfect compromise between what's comfortable for you and easy for her.

Let's take this on the road

As with the previously-learned techniques, start to incorporate 1, 2, 3, Treat into your walks just a little at a time. Choose a point in the walk when your dog is not too excited and there's little distraction around. Feed in the Reward Spot and start counting.

Don't worry that people will think you're batty! They will actually be impressed by your stylish teamwork. You won't be marching along counting for the rest of your days, but you don't want to jettison the counting too soon. It's a prop and a connection to remind your dog to keep checking in with you.

When you're going for that companionable walk, hand-in-hand with a friend, you look about then check back in with them, perhaps to talk. That's what your dog and you will be doing on your walks - enjoying the walk together and checking in with each other.

As you get proficient, you can turn your 1, 2, 3, Treat exercise into normal walking, gradually cutting down the treats as you go - and stopping the counting out loud! Don't rush ahead but consolidate each layer of training before you move on.

More advanced stuff

So the next thing you do is to stop the stopping. You count, - "1, 2, 3, Treat" - touch your leg and feed while moving. Continue this rhythm: "1, 2, 3, Treat," touch your leg, feed while moving, "1, 2, 3, Treat," touch...

Now you are flowing along together, walking rhythmically, smiling happily at each other whenever your dog checks in with you. You're ready to cut back on some of the treats - by counting every other step.

You can count two steps to each number instead of one step. So where you were going: 1, (step) 2, (step) 3, (step) Treat (stop), you are now going: 1, (step, step) 2, (step, step) 3, (step, step) Treat (step, step) ... and so on. Keep a rhythm going.

When this is flowing you can venture out to: 1, (step, step, step) 2, (step, step, step), etc.

If at any time you "lose" your dog, go straight back to the original 1, 2, 3, Treat till she's back with you, then start stretching it out again.

Really advanced stuff

One of the ways to ensure your dog always stays with you is to practice walking at different paces. You've established a suitable pace which stretches out your dog into a trot while allowing you to walk at a comfortable speed. Now you can practice slowing down gradually to a very slow pace, then speeding up again - maybe moving into a slow jog till going back to your normal pace.

The purpose of this is to enable your dog to stay with you, whatever your speed. This will make her more attentive and make the walk more interesting. It can also turn into a great game of "You can't make me go wrong!"

And here's a helpful system to get past attractive smells. Those of you who have already read the second book in this series, *Leave it! How to teach*

Amazing Impulse Control to your Brilliant Family Dog, will recognise this concept. If you haven't read it yet, that joy is still to come!

Lesson 4: Moving past distractions

1. When you're walking along the road and you come to a grassy area which is going to be rivettingly exciting for your dog, just carry on walking past it while your dog says, "I really want to sniff here!"

2. After a few paces, turn back and pass it again. Maybe your dog still strains to get to the grass - keep walking!

3. Now turn again and go past it again. Continue this process.

4. At some stage your dog will realise she's not getting on the grass and will walk nicely with you - BINGO!

5. The moment she decides to stop pulling to get to the grass is the moment you reward her by giving her permission to sniff it. Tell her, "Go sniff!" and give her a minute on the grass.

She's learning that pulling towards something she wants is not going to work, but that if she looks longingly at the grass while keeping with you - maybe, just maybe, she'll get there.

That's not to say you are going to reward her by sending her to sniff at every opportunity! On a walk there are going to be some sniff-points where you can have a break and let her have a mooch around. Dogs don't get to sniff every tree and lamp-post as you walk, but there's no harm in occasionally stopping to admire the "view."

Congratulations on working through this far! You have now found the Holy Grail of dog ownership: *Having your dog walk beside you on a loose lead!*

This is what your dog has now learnt:

- Where she should be in relation to you when on lead
- That she can look around as long as she frequently checks back with you
- Nobody is going to pull her lead, so it's up to her to keep it loose

And you have both learnt:

- Walking with your dog is a pleasurable activity, not a battleground
- It takes two to tango. If you pull, she'll pull
- It takes time to adjust to each other's stride
- "Walks are more fun when I'm not pulling!"

Chapter 6
Complications?

Lacy barks at someone in a funny hat

You are on your way to mastering a system to teach your dog how to walk nicely with you on a loose lead. If your dog is even-tempered and friendly, you're now all set for a lifetime of happy walking - but there are some dogs who have additional issues. These are dogs who have fears and anxieties about the world we live in - maybe they're afraid of people, other dogs, children, joggers, cyclists, traffic, plastic bags, loud noises... You name it, there are dogs who are afraid of it. Known as "Reactive" or "Fearful" dogs, there are an awful lot of them about.

You may not guess from their reaction that they are actually afraid! They are so desperate to keep the thing they fear away from them that they bark ferociously, lunge forward on the end of the lead, and put on an Oscar-winning performance of intimidation and noise that distresses their owner and frightens everybody else.

Maybe you've seen these dogs and wondered why their owners would have such a nasty dog and why they can't control them? Maybe you have one yourself and you know your dog is a devoted, delightful family pet who's brilliant with the children. She's much loved by the whole family - who are baffled about why she does this. And you're at a loss to know how to help her.

If this is you, be assured that there is a way to work with your lovely dog to help her gain confidence so she's no longer at the mercy of her fears popping up in front of her everywhere. It's outside the scope of this book, but there's lots of help for you at

www.brilliantfamilydog.com/growly

Here, you'll find an extensive free course to get you started, all - just like this book and the rest of this Essential Skills series - entirely force-free.

No.1 Tip: Give your dog as much distance as she needs to be able to manage without getting upset

This may be 10 yards, 30 yards, 100 yards, or whatever she needs.

"My dog's friendly!"

If your dog is a paragon of social virtue, a friendly sausage who loves everyone, spare a thought for those who are not so fortunate. It's easy to look down your nose and condemn. Before I knew first-hand what it's like to have a fearful dog I was supercilious myself, but with experience comes understanding and compassion.

The best thing you can do when you see someone struggling with their dog - who in turn appears about to burst into a frenzy of barking - is to give a friendly smile, *lead up your dog*, and head away.

Calling out, "My dog's friendly!" as your loose dog rampages towards the other dog is no help whatever! If this is someone you see regularly, your friendly, non-boisterous dog may indeed be helpful one day to demonstrate to their anxious dog that not all dogs are dangerous, but you need to give the fearful dog as much distance as she needs to be able to cope - only very, *very* gradually getting nearer. This may take the reactive dog months without any help.

With help we're talking about a transformation within weeks.

Direct the struggling owner to www. brilliantfamilydog.com/growly so they can get that help.

The owner of a Growly Dog should expect a gradual improvement rather than an overnight fix. In a month or three they'll be looking back and saying, "Wow! We couldn't have done that calmly before."

No owner or dog has to suffer this level of anxiety and misery - there is light at the end of this tunnel!

In this Chapter you've learnt:

- Not all dogs are created equal
- Fear is a very strong motivator
- "Aggressive" dogs are not usually aggressive
- "Please look after me!"

Conclusion
A new life ahead of us

By the time you've worked through this book, you'll have new systems in place. You and your companion dog will be on the same page! You'll both understand what the other wants. You are now able to look forward to companionable walks without stress and without the danger of being pulled over in the mud, shouting, getting cross, and asking yourself, "Whose idea was it to get a dog?"

You'll be building gradually, keeping in mind that you're going through a complete re-training phase. If you're lucky enough to be starting this with your brand-new puppy you'll never have to re-train! You'll have it right from the start.

While this is going to be the new habit, give your dog time to remember each time where she's meant to be, and keep those rewards flowing freely whenever she does something you like!

Spin-offs

Now your dog walks calmly beside you on a loose lead - instead of head down, scrabbling along the pavement, pulling your arm out - a new world will open up to you. You can take your dog everywhere with you! You'll know that she will behave well on the lead regardless of the distractions. You can walk her with your hands full of shopping bags. You can walk her while you're holding the children's hands and know she'll take care to accommodate them and their erratic speed.

You can enjoy coffee at a café without her lurching about on the lead and putting her paws on the counter. Likewise a drink in a pub will be a pleasant experience once she knows it's her job to keep the lead slack. See *Calm Down! Step-by-step to a Calm, Relaxed, and Brilliant Family Dog* to learn how to get complete peace and quiet while you relax! When you nip out to post a letter your dog can bring you the lead and you'll set off together - rather than you thinking, "Oh no this is too much trouble! I'll go on my own."

You'll be able to enjoy all the things you planned to do when you first got your dog. You'll get fitter, meet more people, shed those pounds, and enjoy the great outdoors. All because you and your dog have learnt a few new skills with the lead.

So your dog will have much more freedom, a more interesting and stimulating life - with visits to beauty spots, nature trails, beaches, the local shops. Most importantly, she will spend much more time with the person who is the most special thing in the world to her:

You.

Top up the learning

Once this is all in place, it will be a simple thing to ensure your dog stays in her Reward Spot. Your hands will be soft on the lead. If she starts to follow her nose away from you, you can simply pause and slow-stop her gently. She'll remember where she should be and pop back beside you. It will take a while for this to become automatic - for both of you. Up till then you are in teaching mode.

Appreciation

I want to offer thanks to all those who have helped me get where I am with my dogs:

- First of all, my own long-suffering dogs! They have taught me so much when I've taken the time to listen.

- My students, who have shown me how they learn best, enabling me to give them what they need to know in a way that works for them.

- Some legendary teachers, principal amongst them: Sue Ailsby, Leslie McDevitt, Grisha Stewart, Susan Garrett. I wholeheartedly recommend them. They are trailblazers.

Resources

If you've enjoyed learning this key skill and you want to find the other three parts of the puzzle, go to www.brilliantfamilydog.com/books and pick up your next book!

Calm Down! *Step-by-Step to a Calm, Relaxed, and Brilliant Family Dog - Book 1*

Leave It! *How to teach Amazing Impulse Control to your Brilliant Family Dog - Book 2*

Here Boy! *Step-by-Step to a Stunning Recall from your Brilliant Family Dog - Book 4*

These cover the four skills you need to turn your wild puppy into your Brilliant Family Dog.

Meanwhile, for more free training, go to www.brilliantfamilydog.com and get a series of instructional emails on common day-to-day problems, like jumping up, chewing, barking, and so on.

Thank you so very much for all your excellent advice. *Lisa*

I just wanted to drop you a quick line to say how great your emails are. There are always a few lines in each one which are corkers! Fluffy pup / piranha fish, well yes, that I know now! It's also so nice to know that this is normal. *Laura and Waffle*

Just to let you know that Molly is progressing really well thanks to your tips. *Anne and Molly*

I really appreciate your emails: they are very helpful! *Norma and Tonto*

And www.brilliantfamilydog.com/growly is for those of you with anxious and fearful dogs.

And if you've got any specific queries, you can email me direct at beverley@brilliantfamilydog.com This will come straight to my personal inbox and I'll answer you - usually within 48 hours. Try me!

Harness

www.goodfordogs.co.uk/products for UK and Europe (see video)

I supply these harnesses to the British Isles and Europe. If you get one through me I will benefit financially but it won't cost you any more. Watch the video. If you can find another harness that has the same effect, go for it!

http://2houndswholesale.com/Where-to-Buy.html for the rest of the world

http://dogmantics.com/is-it-harmful-to-attach-a-leash-to-your-dogs-neck-2

You can get a hands-free lead which fixes round the hips if you want to do jogging, skijoring, and canicross with your dog.

For Challenging Dogs

www.brilliantfamilydog.com/growly
www.goodfordogs.co.uk/aggressive-dogs.html
www.fearfuldogs.com
www.controlunleashed.net

Your free book is waiting for you!

Get the next piece of the puzzle

Get the second book in this series absolutely free at

www.brilliantfamilydog.com/freebook

About the author

I've been training dogs for many years. First for competitive dog sports and over time to be stellar family pets. For most of my life, I've lived with up to four dogs, so I'm well used to getting a multi-dog household to run smoothly. It soon became clear that a force-free approach was by far the most successful, effective, and rewarding for me and the dogs. I've done the necessary studying for my various qualifications - for rehab of anxious and fearful "aggressive" dogs, early puppy development, and learning theory and its practical applications. I am continually studying and learning this endlessly amazing subject!

There are some superb teachers and advocates of force-free dog training, and you'll find those I am particularly indebted to in the Resources Section. Some of the methods I show you are well-known in the force-free dog training community, while many have my own particular twist.

A lot of my learning has come through the Puppy Classes, Puppy Walks, and Starter Classes I teach. These dog-owners are not looking for competition-standard training; they just want a Brilliant Family Dog they can take anywhere. Working with real dogs and their real owners keeps me humble - and resourceful! It's no good being brilliant at training dogs if you can't convey this enthusiasm and knowledge to the person the dog has to live with. So I'm grateful for everything my students have taught me about how they learn best.

Beverley Courtney BA(Hons) CBATI CAP2 MAPDT(UK) PPG

CPSIA information can be obtained
at www.ICGtesting.com
Printed in the USA
BVHW080413070721
611240BV00011B/1506